THE CROSS

AND THE MEANING OF EASTER

JONATHAN GRIFFITHS

First published in Great Britain in 2022

British Library Cataloguing in Publication Data
A record for this book is available from the British Library

ISBN: 978-1-914966-43-9

Designed and typeset by Pete Barnsley (CreativeHoot.com)

Printed in Denmark by Nørhaven

10Publishing, a division of 10ofthose.com

Unit C, Tomlinson Road, Leyland, PR25 2DY, England

Email: info@10ofthose.com
Website: www.10ofthose.com

3 5 7 10 8 6 4 2

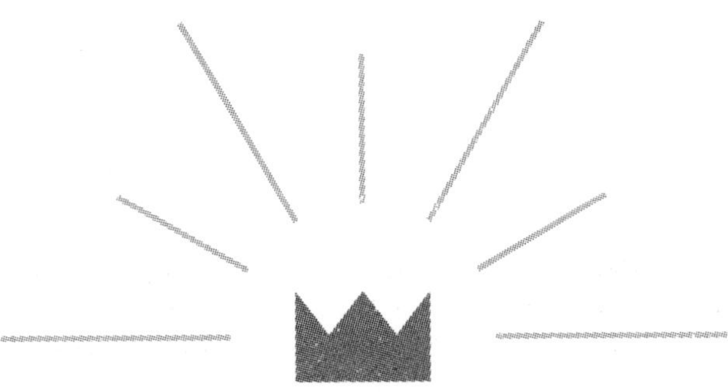

CONTENTS

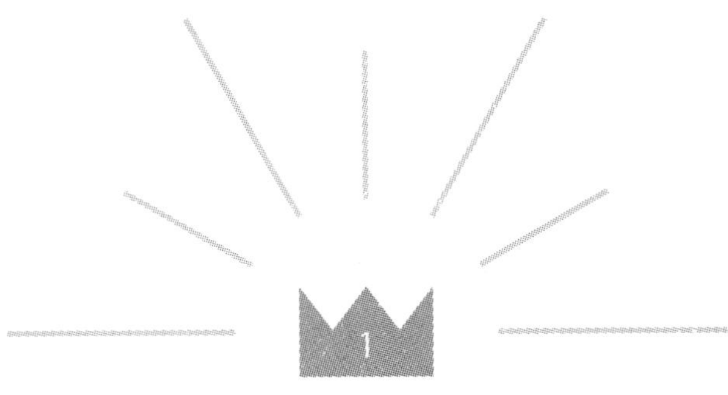

WHO IS IN CONTROL?

We all know the panic of a crisis. A cursory glance at recent history teaches us the result and impact of economic collapse, violent war, political insecurity, and global pandemic. In these moments of crisis, our eyes turn to world leaders in the hope that they will be able to give us an answer or solution. We tune into the news briefings of politicians that we might have previously ignored, now hanging on their every word.

Yet however good their efforts are, however hard they try, they know (and we know) that their ability to control a crisis is incredibly limited. There is only so much they can do. Faced with an impossible situation, human leaders are finite in power and insight. That is not a criticism; that is just hard reality.

So, if presidents and prime ministers are not in control, then who is? Many of us have cause to ask this question in times of crisis and unrest.

The very same question stands at the heart of Easter. The story of a crucified man who rose from the dead may be familiar to us, but, as a result, we can easily miss or overlook what it is really all about. Despite all appearances to the contrary, the man who died on Good Friday and rose again three days later is really the true ruler of all things. Jesus is the one in supreme control, even at the very moment when things seem most out of control.

It may feel as if our present days are dark. Recent years have brought true crisis and catastrophe to so many in our unsettled world. But as we enter into the Easter story once more, we are, in fact, entering into the account of the very darkest days the world has ever known. It is precisely in this moment of darkness and chaos that the Bible shows us the true authority of Jesus Christ.

Who is in control? To answer that question we simply need to immerse ourselves in the Easter narrative, to look at its key characters, and to allow the story to unfold on its own terms.

2

THE TRIAL

Then they led Jesus from the house of Caiaphas to the governor's headquarters. It was early morning. They themselves did not enter the governor's headquarters, so that they would not be defiled, but could eat the Passover. So Pilate went outside to them and said, "What accusation do you bring against this man?" They answered him, "If this man were not doing evil, we would not have delivered him over to you." Pilate said to them, "Take him yourselves and judge him by your own law." The Jews said to him, "It is not lawful for us to put anyone to death." This was to fulfill the word that Jesus had spoken to show by what kind of death he was going to die.

So Pilate entered his headquarters again and called Jesus and said to him, "Are you the King of the Jews?" Jesus answered, "Do you say this of your own accord, or did others say it to you about me?" Pilate answered, "Am I a Jew? Your own nation and the chief priests have delivered you over to me. What have you done?" Jesus answered, "My kingdom is not of this world. If my kingdom were of this world, my servants would have been fighting, that I might not be delivered over to the Jews. But my kingdom is not from the world." Then Pilate said to him, "So you are a king?" Jesus answered, "You say that I am a king. For this purpose I was born and for this purpose I have come into the world—to bear witness to the truth. Everyone who is of the truth listens to my voice." Pilate said to him, "What is truth?"

After he had said this, he went back outside to the Jews and told them, "I find no guilt in him. But you have a custom that I should release one man for you at the Passover. So do you want me to release to you the King of the Jews?" They cried out again, "Not this man, but Barabbas!" Now Barabbas was a robber.

Then Pilate took Jesus and flogged him. And the soldiers twisted together a crown of thorns and put it on his head and arrayed him in a purple robe. They came up to him, saying, "Hail, King of the Jews!" and struck him with their hands. Pilate went out again and said to them, "See, I am bringing him out to you that you may know that I find no guilt in him." So Jesus came out, wearing the crown of thorns and the purple robe. Pilate said to them, "Behold the man!" When the chief priests and the officers saw him, they cried out, "Crucify him, crucify him!" Pilate said to them, "Take him yourselves and crucify him, for I find no guilt in him." The Jews answered him, "We have a law, and according to that law he ought to die because he has made himself the Son of God." When Pilate heard this statement, he was even more afraid. He entered his headquarters again and said to Jesus, "Where are you from?" But Jesus gave him no answer. So Pilate said to him, "You will not speak to me? Do you not know that I have authority to release you and authority to crucify you?" Jesus answered him, "You would have no authority over me at all unless it had been given you from above. Therefore he who delivered me over to you has the greater sin."

From then on Pilate sought to release him, but the Jews cried out, "If you release this man, you are not Caesar's friend. Everyone who makes himself a king opposes Caesar." So when Pilate heard these words, he brought Jesus out and sat down on the judgment seat at a place called The Stone Pavement, and in Aramaic Gabbatha. Now it was the day of Preparation of the Passover. It was about the sixth hour. He said to the Jews, "Behold your King!" They cried out, "Away with him, away with him, crucify him!" Pilate said to them, "Shall I crucify your King?" The chief priests answered, "We have no king but Caesar." So he delivered him over to them to be crucified (John 18:28 – 19:16).

We join the story at a crucial and dramatic moment. Jesus has eaten his "last" supper with his followers. He has gone to pray in the Garden of Gethsemane, where Judas—one of his followers—betrayed him. He has been taken to the religious authorities. He has been renounced by Peter, another of his followers. He has stood before Caiaphas, the high priest. And now he is before Pilate, the Roman Governor—the regional representative of the most powerful empire the earth has ever known.

The crowd of Jesus' accusers are from the religious establishment. They had led him to the governor's headquarters because they did not have the power to execute an individual. They needed the Roman ruler to give the order.

It is early in the morning, perhaps before six o'clock—this is probably not how Pilate wants to start his day. Jesus is taken inside the building. The crowd remain outside. They do not want to be ceremonially defiled by entering a Roman building the night before the Passover, their biggest religious festival.

Pilate, of course, has not sought out this situation. But his is the burden of leadership, and so now he has to deal with it. And in doing so, he is placed in the rather undignified position of having to scurry between Jesus, who is inside, and the crowd, who are outside. Like a waiter scuttling between tables and the kitchen on a busy evening, Pilate rushes out to the crowd and asks a very reasonable question: "What accusation do you bring against this man?"

The crowd have nothing substantial to say: "If this man were not doing evil, we would not have delivered him over to you."

Pilate has the good sense to see that this is nonsense. He asks the religious leaders to take Jesus away and deal with the situation themselves. But they quickly get to the heart of the matter. You Romans took that power from us, they say. We want the death penalty for this man, and we will not settle for anything less.

Pilate now makes the run back inside—perhaps he has to lift his toga to avoid tripping as he goes—and asks Jesus the question that all Jerusalem is asking: "Are you the King of the Jews?"

Jesus does not give him the satisfaction of a direct answer.

But Pilate knows that if Jesus will admit to making a claim to royal power, then that will simplify the issue. Rome would not tolerate anyone claiming to be king. That would give the grounds needed for a swift execution. Baiting him further, Pilate asks, "So you are a king?"

Jesus answers, "You say that I am a king. For this purpose I was born and for this purpose I have come into the world—to bear witness to the truth. Everyone who is of the truth listens to my voice."

These are profound claims. Rather than allowing the conversation simply to be about politics, Jesus moves to a higher level: this is about universal questions of ultimate significance; this is about *truth*. Jesus has come to bear witness to truth, even insisting that he is the authority on truth.

Jesus' claims are massive, but rather than grapple with them honestly, Pilate simply waives aside the issue. "What is truth?" he asks.

On the face of it, the question is enormous, to be sure. But for Pilate it is little more than an avoidance strategy. He takes himself back outside to the fresh morning air and the waiting crowd, and declares that he finds Jesus not guilty.

To us, as observers, this might sound good. There has been some progress in the trial, we think. Despite his shallow examination, Pilate has actually come to the truth. *You are right, Pilate. Now let this innocent man go.* Surely any just ruler lets a prisoner go free who he realizes is not guilty. Well, not this time. Not with this changeable ruler.

In fact, Pilate's next breath confirms that he is both weak and lacking integrity: "But you have a custom that I should release one man for you at the Passover. So do you want me to release to you the King of the Jews [that is, Jesus]?"

The crowd play on Pilate's lack of leadership and cry out for a man named Barabbas—a robber, a domestic terrorist, an utter and complete danger to society—to be released instead. The crowd have cast their vote. They want Barabbas, not Jesus.

Having received instruction from his subjects, Pilate goes back inside and orders Jesus to be flogged, mocked, and beaten. But Pilate completely lacks both direction and conviction, so he comes back out and makes the following bizarre pronouncement: "See, I am bringing him out to you that you may know that I find no guilt in him." Having punished and humiliated Jesus, Pilate again declares him innocent.

The crowd is not appeased. The chief priests and officers cry out, "Crucify him! Crucify him!"

In feeble abdication of his responsibility, Pilate says, "Take him yourselves and crucify him, for I find no guilt in him."

Here is a judge who does not want to try the case. Here is a ruler who does not want to give the decree. He is like the child who hopes the problem will go away if he closes his eyes and firmly inserts his fingers in his ears.

But the crowd are insistent. They answer that, according to their law, Jesus deserves the death penalty because he claimed to be the Son of God. This makes Pilate afraid on two counts. He clearly does not want to kill Jesus—if the claim is true, he risks killing someone of divine origin. Nor does he want to upset the crowd and create a political headache. And so an ostensibly powerful leader becomes paralyzed by fear.

Making the trip back inside—no doubt tired of pacing back and forth between the balcony and the inner courtyard—Pilate asks Jesus, "Where are you from?"

Jesus declines to answer, which seems to unsettle Pilate further.

"Do you not know that I have authority to release you and authority to crucify you?" he says.

And then Jesus tells Pilate plainly that he would have no authority over him had not God given it to him first.

Pilate is sobered by all of this. He clearly recognizes Jesus' innocence but also, perhaps, something of his true identity. So he tries, yet again, to release him. But the crowd will not have it. They say that letting Jesus go would be treason and a betrayal of Caesar. Clearly wearied and conflicted, Pilate sits down on what is described as the judgment seat. He presents Jesus to the crowd as their king. They demand crucifixion. They insist Caesar is their true king. And the passage ends with these simple but sobering words: "So he delivered him over to them to be crucified."

These events are some of the darkest and most tragic to be found on all the pages of human history. Any sympathetic reader of the narrative has to ache for justice to be done—for Jesus Christ, the innocent and humble man, to be shown decency and justice. But the scene is only made darker by Pilate's failure to lead. Even the drama and choreography of Pilate scurrying back and forth between the crowd outside and the prisoner inside highlights for us the extent to which Pilate is not actually in control. Yet through Pilate's weakness and lack of leadership, the narrative points us to an altogether different kind of ruler.

A CRUCIFIED KING

You must have noticed that Jesus is notably quiet as these proceedings unfold. He seems to stay in one place, unmoved, as Pilate scurries around his headquarters. But increasingly, and by degree, we see how Jesus' stately composure speaks of his true authority.

The first hint comes when John (the author of the story) tells us that the religious leaders, who so want Jesus dead, have brought him to Pilate so that he might sentence him. They did not have the legal authority to sentence anyone to death. If they did, their method would have been stoning. But they probably preferred to see the more dramatic Roman punishment of crucifixion. As they argue and cajole for this,

John simply tells us, "This was to fulfil the word that Jesus had spoken to show by what kind of death he was going to die."

Earlier in John's story, Jesus predicted that he would be lifted up from the earth (John 12:32). In other words, he knew that he would be crucified. In fact, he *planned* that he would be crucified.

The Jewish religious law, which the people of Jesus' time followed, said that a person who is hung on a tree bears the curse of God. Jesus came that he might die that way to bear the curse of God *for* the people. That was his plan. That was his intention. Despite the ugly machinations of the crowds and the dithering of Pilate, everything was unfolding in order that the word that Jesus had spoken would be fulfilled.

Jesus is the prisoner on trial, yes, but at the same time he is the ruler who reigns. He came to earth to die—and to die in that particular way. It was no cosmic accident. It was the will and intention of the cosmic ruler, the Son of God himself.

It is no mistake that Pilate raises the question of Jesus' authority at this point. He asks outright, "Are you the King of the Jews?"

Jesus does not give him a direct answer but, when pressed, says, "My kingdom is not of this world."

Jesus does not deny his power, but he does tell Pilate that his kingdom is not like that of Caesar. His rule does not operate on the same principles. His authority is not presently seen in physical, military, or geographical terms. The authority of Jesus comes from God and is shown in a way that neither Pilate nor the crowd can recognize.

As Jesus explains, "For this purpose I was born and for this purpose I have come into the world—to bear witness to the truth. Everyone who is of the truth listens to my voice."

Jesus the Messiah did not come into the world wielding a sword or a sceptre, but proclaiming a message of truth. He spent his earthly life telling others that message—that humanity stands guilty of ignoring and side-lining God, and that only he can bring forgiveness and life to this needy world.

The very trial at which Jesus stands, and which will lead to his death, will become the means by which he will fulfill his word. Pilate cannot see this. The crowds do not understand it. But Jesus' unjust death will be the mechanism by which he saves all those who believe in him.

THE TRUE KING

As we read and observe the trial scene, we realize that the narrative is laden with irony. It betrays more truth than any of the actors within it know, save Jesus himself. Mockingly dressed as a king and crowned with an instrument of humiliation and torture, Jesus is presented to the public—not for praise, but for abuse. Though no one there realizes as much, it is through this very mockery, suffering, and rejection that Jesus enters into his kingly calling. He will establish his kingdom and lead his subjects from a cross, not a chariot. He must go through these agonies to save his people and secure his kingdom. This breaks the mould and confounds every expectation, but what we read in the narrative is actually the regal presentation of the true King. This bruised and beaten man is God's appointed Messiah, his saving King, for all who will believe.

The tables are turned. Something within Pilate has caused him to fear what he is doing. Jesus is bolder and clearer in what he says, declaring to Pilate that *his* authority is only delegated. Pilate might think he is running the show, but the unseen hand of God is overruling everything. This is heaven's plan, not Rome's. This is God's will, not the crowd's. The decision lies with the divine ruler. The true King is not Caesar or his representative; it is the one who bears the crown of thorns.

In his weakness and folly, Pilate prepares to have Jesus killed, but he does so while declaring that Jesus is the King. "Shall I crucify your King?" he asks the crowd.

Yes, is the answer that returns.

As Pilate delivers *this* King to be crucified, little does he know that Jesus must enter into his kingdom by way of the cross. The innocent King before him will bring salvation to a guilty people. The King will die so that they may go free.

THE CROWD

The story of the crowd is a cautionary one. They came in a spirit of inexplicable hatred, baying for blood. As we watch their interactions with Jesus, they reveal so much of the human heart in rebellion against God. The crowd wants

Barabbas to be released, not because they like him, but because their hostility to Jesus runs so deep. There is no explanation that makes real sense of this incredible choice, except that it reflects a pattern of human behaviour and the fixed preference of our human hearts. There is something about Jesus that the darkness of the human heart recoils from and rebels against. *No, not this man. Give us Barabbas.*

That same choice is before us today. Will you recognize this meek and humble King who comes with the message of truth? Will you see in his suffering and death his plan to save? Will you submit to his rule and trust his salvation?

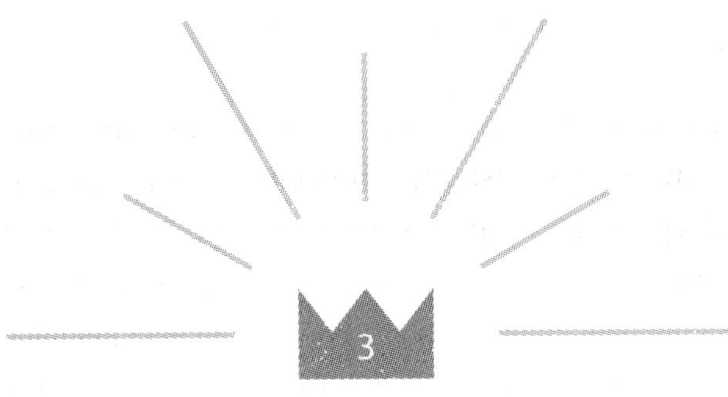

THE ARCHITECT'S PLAN

After this, Jesus, knowing that all was now finished, said (to fulfill the Scripture), "I thirst." A jar full of sour wine stood there, so they put a sponge full of the sour wine on a hyssop branch and held it to his mouth. When Jesus had received the sour wine, he said, "It is finished," and he bowed his head and gave up his spirit (John 19:28–30).

You have probably lived through a major construction project at some point. Maybe a road in your commute was rebuilt; maybe the office on which you work was upgraded in a major way; maybe you have had a significant home renovation. Some of my earliest childhood memories are of our house being rebuilt. My parents undertook a major building project when I was three years old, and decided that we would try to live in the house while it was all happening. (I think they perhaps came to regret that decision a little bit!)

When walls are being torn down and holes are being dug, when there is mud and dust and chaos everywhere, most construction sites look like a complete disaster zone. *Surely this is all one big mistake? Surely this situation was brought about by a terrible accident rather than an architect's plan?* It is a great help in that chaotic time to look back and see the architect's drawings. When you look at their plan, you receive assurance that the apparent chaos and mess are intentional and purposeful—and not, in fact, accidental.

Here in John's account of the Easter story, he refers us back to the architect's plan. He points us back to the Old Testament Scriptures and to the pattern that was set there for the promised Messiah. Notice the way in which he highlights this for us: "After this, Jesus, knowing that all was now finished, said (to fulfill the Scripture), 'I thirst.'"

In writing this way, John is taking us back to a particular Old Testament passage, Psalm 22. This was written centuries before the birth of Jesus by King David, the most famous Old Testament king. David opens with, "My God, my God, why have you forsaken me?" He later continues, "All who see me mock me; they make mouths at me; they wag their heads." David then describes his experience of going through terrible suffering, torturous abuse, and mocking, to the very point of death.

However, the psalm moves on and David describes how he will praise God in the company of God's people. More than that, people from all over the earth will turn to God, worship him, and proclaim his righteousness to future generations. In short, suffering will lead to victory, to the assembling of a great congregation, to a massive turning of people to God—and all for God's praise and glory.

Yet, whatever suffering David experienced, it was not the full measure described in this psalm. Inspired by God's Spirit, he spoke of an experience beyond his own. John sees that David's words point to Jesus, the King who suffered unjustly for his people, so that he might gather a people from the ends of the earth and save them for his glory.

John wants us to know that the mess of Good Friday was set down plainly in the architect's plan, all those centuries before. Yes, it looks like a disaster, but it is in fact a grand project reaching its glorious culmination. The dust will settle and the design will be seen in all its beauty and wonder.

THE TRUE KING FINISHES HIS WORK

Jesus lets out a heartfelt cry as he dies: "It is finished!" It is all over ... ! To our ears, that cry could be taken in two different ways. On the one hand, it could be understood as a concession of failure and a cry of defeat. It could be heard as an expression of despair over a life tragically cut short and an admission that goals will never be reached. We might liken the mood to the time when a promising venture goes bankrupt. The CEO pores over the books in his office and then concedes to his team through tears, "It's all over, the dream is dead!"

Yet, in a different context, the very same cry could be heard as a declaration of success. Picture a surgeon standing at the operating table after a gruelling procedure, with the final stitch sewn, and the vital signs stable: "It is finished." Or the student submitting their dissertation after years of work: "It is finished." Or the builder putting the final finishing detail on the new house with a glow of satisfaction: "It is finished."

As Jesus recognizes that his saving work is finished, he makes a declaration of victory, not a concession of defeat. The word he uses, in the original language, refers to reaching a goal or landing on a target—and this is exactly what has taken place.

The great surprise and paradox of the cross is that what looks like terrible defeat and crushing disappointment for Jesus' followers is actually the great culmination and victory. The cross was the completion of Jesus' mission, not the moment when it was ruined.

To see that, we need to understand not just what was predicted about the suffering King in the Old Testament, but also what Jesus said during his time on earth.

Earlier in John's Gospel, as Jesus anticipates being lifted up on the cross, he tells one nervous enquirer:

> *And as Moses lifted up the serpent in the wilderness, so must the Son of Man be lifted up, that whoever believes in him may have eternal life" (John 3:14–15).*

Then, a little later, Jesus speaks of his intention to lay down his life for his people:

> *I am the good shepherd. I know my own and my own know me, just as the Father knows me and I know the Father; and I lay down my life for the sheep. ... No one takes it from me, but I lay it down of my own accord. I have authority to lay it down and I have authority to take it up again (John 10:14–15, 18).*

Again, even as the cross draws nearer, Jesus declares:

> *Now is my soul troubled. And what shall I say? 'Father, save me from this hour'? But for*

> *this purpose I have come to this hour. Father, glorify your name. ... And I, when I am lifted up from the earth, will draw all people to myself (John 12:27–28, 32).*

When Jesus is eventually lifted up on the cross, it is because he willingly lays down his life for his sheep. He does this to glorify the Father by giving eternal life to all who believe. As Jesus hangs on that cross, he speaks a declaration of victory and not defeat, a cry of completion and not of failure. "It is finished," he says.

These words have echoed down the centuries. They come to us today as good news. They tell us that all the work needed to pay the price of our rebellion against God is *finished*. Salvation is accomplished, fully and finally. It is ours simply to trust in Jesus' saving work and to give thanks to the One who suffered in our place.

It may be that you are reading this book with a heavy heart, one weighed down by guilt because of the wrong things you have thought or said or done. Perhaps you are frightened, knowing that you can never make your relationship with God right by yourself.

The message of Easter is good news for you. It is, in fact, the best news the world has ever heard. The price of our rebellion has been paid at the cross and forgiveness is freely available. We could never pay the debt ourselves, but we can receive the gift of the finished work of Jesus on our behalf. For all who receive that gift by faith, there is complete pardon and full assurance. You can know freedom from the guilt of sin and release from its burden. The opportunity is here, even today, to come by faith to the One who died on the cross and to receive full forgiveness because the work is finished.

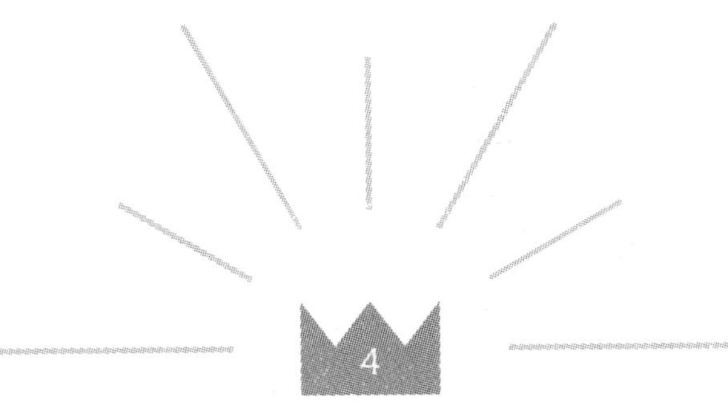

LIFE!

Now on the first day of the week Mary Magdalene came to the tomb early, while it was still dark, and saw that the stone had been taken away from the tomb. So she ran and went to Simon Peter and the other disciple, the one whom Jesus loved, and said to them, "They have taken the Lord out of the tomb, and we do not know where they have laid him." ... Simon Peter ... went into the tomb. He saw the linen cloths lying there, and the face cloth, which had been on Jesus' head, not lying with the linen cloths but folded up in a place by itself. Then the other disciple, who had reached the tomb first, also went in, and he saw and believed; for as yet they did not understand the Scripture, that he must rise from the dead. Then the disciples went back to their homes.

But Mary stood weeping outside the tomb ... and saw Jesus standing, but she did not know that it was Jesus. Jesus said to her, "Woman, why are you weeping? Whom are you seeking?" Supposing him to be the gardener, she said to him, "Sir, if you have carried him away, tell me where you have laid him, and I will take him away." Jesus said to her, "Mary." She turned and said to him in Aramaic, "Rabboni!" (which means Teacher). Jesus said to her, "Do not cling to me, for I have not yet ascended to the Father; but go to my brothers and say to them, 'I am ascending to my Father and your Father, to my God and your God.'" Mary Magdalene went and announced to the disciples, "I have seen the Lord"—and that he had said these things to her.

On the evening of that day, the first day of the week, the doors being locked where the

> *disciples were for fear of the Jews, Jesus came and stood among them and said to them, "Peace be with you." When he had said this, he showed them his hands and his side. Then the disciples were glad when they saw the Lord" (John 20:1–20).*

Our generation has lived through the most fearful pandemic the world has seen in a century or more. Comfortable illusions of virtual immortality—offered by modern medicine and universal health care—have been unceremoniously shattered and swept away. The world's most gifted scientists have been confounded, at least for a time, by an invisible virus. The best hospitals of the greatest cities have been overwhelmed. Rich and powerful nations around the world have cried out for basic supplies that they could not procure for any price. And we have all been forced to confront the ugly reality of death.

I have no idea, of course, what type of situations you faced during this time. But I cannot help but wonder if you will have picked up this book exactly because of the impact of the pandemic or another crisis or trial. The fearful reality of death that filled our newsfeeds and TV screens, and perhaps even touched you quite personally, has maybe prompted you to think more seriously about spiritual realities. In short: you are looking for hope and you are wondering, maybe in a way you never have before, whether the Christian message holds hope for you.

If that is where you are, then I am especially glad you are reading this. We all need to receive hope. As we look at what happens after Jesus' death on the cross, we receive the joyful news that Jesus Christ offers the concrete hope of eternal life.

DOUBTS ANSWERED

We have already considered the lead-up to Jesus' crucifixion and his death on Good Friday. In this chapter, I want to pick up the story early on the Sunday morning. Mary Magdalene, a faithful follower of Jesus who had stood by him at the cross, comes to the tomb where he has been laid. However, she finds that the great stone, which had sealed the tomb, has been rolled away and the tomb itself is empty. Bewildered and concerned, she runs to get the other disciples. Two of them come to look. They find within the tomb the linen burial clothes, but no body.

Of course, it is important to remember that these devastated disciples did not have a full understanding of what was happening. They had listened to Jesus speak about his death and his resurrection, but the penny really had not yet dropped. And so, when Jesus was arrested and put on trial, most of them abandoned him in fear and confusion. They thought it was all over. They had not understood that his intention was both to die and to rise. But now, suddenly, one of the disciples (many think that this is perhaps John himself) realizes: "Then the other disciple, who had reached the tomb first, also went in, and he saw and believed."

The other disciples go home, but Mary Magdalene stays standing at the tomb weeping. She has not yet understood that Jesus is alive. To her, the tragedy of his death has been compounded by the theft of his body. But then a man appears. Mary thinks he is the gardener until he says her name, at which point she recognizes him. It is Jesus. She runs and, in joy and amazement, tells the other disciples, "I have seen the Lord."

In the next scene, we see the disciples gathered in a house, cowering with the doors locked. The religious leaders had lobbied to put Jesus to death only days ago, and the disciples think they might be next. Into the midst of this fearful situation, Jesus appears and speaks to them. He shows them his hands and his side, which still bear the wounds of the cross, even now, in resurrection life.

One of the disciples, a man named Thomas, was missing from this gathering. He ends up having his own unique experience of the risen Jesus, and this is where we next pick up the story:

> *Now Thomas, one of the twelve, called the Twin, was not with them when Jesus came. So the other disciples told him, "We have seen the Lord." But he said to them, "Unless I see in his hands the mark of the nails, and place my*

> *finger into the mark of the nails, and place my hand into his side, I will never believe."*
>
> *Eight days later, his disciples were inside again, and Thomas was with them. Although the doors were locked, Jesus came and stood among them and said, "Peace be with you." Then he said to Thomas, "Put your finger here, and see my hands; and put out your hand, and place it in my side. Do not disbelieve, but believe." Thomas answered him, "My Lord and my God!" Jesus said to him, "Have you believed because you have seen me? Blessed are those who have not seen and yet have believed" (John 20:24–31).*

Thomas is not there when Jesus first appears to the others in that locked room. He only hears about the resurrection of Jesus second-hand. For Thomas, this is not good enough. It is all just too much to contemplate and accept—Jesus, dead on Friday, but alive on Sunday. So Thomas speaks the words that have made him famous as "doubting Thomas": "Unless I see in his hands the mark of the nails, and place my finger into the mark of the nails, and place my hand into his side, I will never believe."

Now, it is easy to be hard on Thomas, but the truth is that the other disciples were in a position of relative advantage: they were able to see before they believed. I think we can understand, on some level, how Thomas felt. After all, the miracle of a dead man rising to life is kind of a huge deal.

Eight days go by, and the disciples are back in the room with the doors locked, still frightened for their lives. This time Thomas is there. Jesus appears to them again, and again says to them, "Peace be with you." Jesus could have given Thomas a hard time for his failure to believe based on the testimony of the others, but Jesus is so kind and so patient. He invites Thomas to observe the evidence for himself—the evidence that he demanded: to touch his hands and his side—and believe. It seems as though Thomas stops short of doing that. Simply seeing the evidence before him, he answers with a powerful confession of faith, "My Lord and my God!"

OUR GREATEST NEED

At this point, John, the author, moves out of the background. He stops being the narrator of the story, instead stepping into the foreground to tell us why he has written his book. He explains how he, as an eyewitness of Jesus' life, intends to be part of our process of belief:

> *Now Jesus did many other signs in the presence of the disciples, which are not written in this book; but these are written so that you may believe that Jesus is the Christ, the Son of God, and that by believing you may have life in his name (John 20:30–31).*

Jesus did so much in his earthly ministry. He performed so many miracles that were signs for us of his identity and his mission. But, John says, I have written this much down so that you may believe, and by believing have eternal life in his name.

From our vantage point 2,000 years after the historical events of Easter, you and I do not have access to the visible, physical evidence of the resurrection. The risen Jesus is now in heaven. But here is what we do have before us: we have the testimony of John and others that Jesus rose again. And if we believe their testimony, we will have life. *This* is the point of the Easter story.

For centuries before Jesus came to earth as a man, God had promised that he would send a saving King into the world who would be his own Son. This Messiah would liberate his people from slavery and bring them into a truly glorious future.

Those living in Jesus' day thought their Messiah would come and liberate them from Roman oppression. They expected the Messiah to lead them into a future that would be glorious in national and military terms. Jesus came and claimed to be God's saving King, but did not take up the sword or set out a political vision. The religious people therefore did not know what to do with him. In fact, they eventually rejected him to the point of having him executed on the cross.

In all this, what they failed to see was this: God's plan for his saving King was not so meagre as for him merely to bring about a political or military revolution. God's plan was far greater.

His Son would come and liberate humanity from its deepest bondage and address its most profound need.

The Bible tells us that the root cause of all suffering and all pain in this world is the fact that we have turned from God to live our own way, without reference to him. We have become alienated from him; we have invited his judgment for the evil things that we have done; and we experience the fruit of that rebellion as the beauty of life ends again and again in the tragedy of the grave. That is, in short, our deepest need; that is our greatest problem. We are a people who were created to live, but because of our sin, we are destined to die.

God's plan was for his Messiah to come and pay the price of that rebellion, bear the judgment for sin at the cross, and then rise again in victory over the grave. What John wants us to see and believe is that this Jesus is indeed the promised Christ, the long-awaited Saviour.

I sometimes have some background music playing on YouTube when I am working. I find the music can be helpful, but occasionally I have to endure the ads, which punctuate the playlist and can be a real distraction. For a while, one ad that kept popping up was of someone who promised that he could teach anyone to sing. The gist of it was basically that he is a great singer, who figured out how to sing well, and he has now an impressive track record of teaching other people to sing like opera stars. There are ads for other similar things on there. Perhaps you've seen them: *I figured out how to write a bestselling novel—I can teach you how. I went from couch potato to weightlifting star—I can get you there in six weeks.* But how do we know whether we can believe their claims?

Jesus Christ has conquered the grave. He has fulfilled God's plan. Here is the eyewitness account to prove it. And the offer of the gospel—the offer of Easter—is simply this: Jesus can carry *us* through the grave to eternal life. Having died on the cross, Jesus appeared to eyewitnesses and showed himself to be alive. He offers the blessing of eternal life to those who believe. *That* is the real hope that we all need.

I cannot offer you a cure from the pandemics and crises that this world throws in our path. Anyone who pretends that they can is lying to you. But on the basis of God's word, here is what is on offer to you today: life in Jesus' name. It is the offer of resurrection life beyond the grave because Jesus died for your sin and rose again three days later.

Will you believe in him today? Will you turn from your sinful rebellion against him, and will you trust him with your life and with your death? John tells us—in fact, he promises us—that we will have life through believing that this risen Jesus is the Christ, the Son of God. Will you believe that, even today?

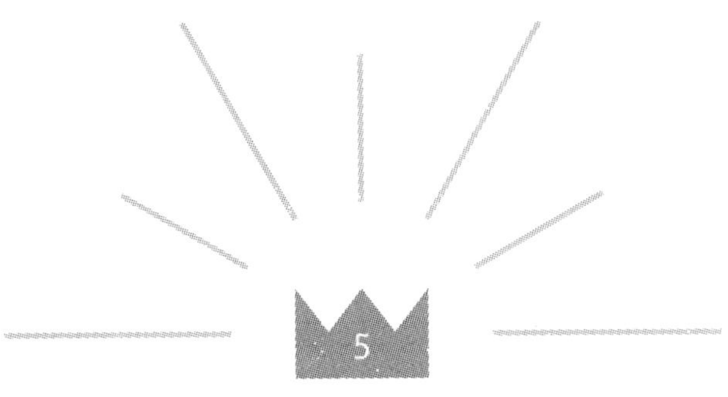

WHAT NEXT?

We all have to confront the ultimate question of who is truly in charge of the world. That question comes pressing upon us in an urgent way in times of crisis and in days of panic. But, whatever the season or circumstance, the question remains—and each of us has to reckon with it personally.

Jesus Christ came into this world as God's promised saving King of humanity. He came in humility to suffer and die. Despite how it may have appeared initially, he came to be the true Judge and heaven's King. He offers us forgiveness through his death on the cross, and life by his resurrection from the dead. John tells us that he wrote his account of the life, death, and resurrection of Jesus "so that you may believe that Jesus is the Christ, the Son of God, and that by believing you may have life in his name" (John 20:31).

The question for each of us, then, is simply this: will you believe that Jesus is the Christ, the Son of God, and so receive life in his name? To believe in him requires us to recognize that our attitude toward him has been wrong; that we are guilty of rejecting him and the Father who sent him. It means accepting that John's testimony about him is true; it means recognizing that the crowds were wrong.

Are you ready to respond to him in this way? If so, you might like to make the words of this prayer your own:

Lord Jesus Christ, I am sorry that I have rejected you in my life. I want to say that I believe that you are the Christ, the Saviour, heaven's King. Thank you for dying on the cross to pay the price of my sin. Please forgive me for all the wrong I have done and for my failure to honour you as King. Please give me the gift of life in your name. Amen.